S0-AHR-441

BODIES OF LIGHTNING

11-1-95

For Reba Stitt

All best wishes. Enjoyed

seeing you in Salisbury!

Alan Britt

Bodies of Lightning

by Alan Britt

CypressBooks

San Mateo, California

ACKNOWLEDGMENTS

The author is grateful to the editors of the following publications, who published most of these poems:

Anathema Review, Art/Life, Black Buzzard Review, Black Moon, Blackwater, Blank Gun Silencer, Chariton Review, Glass Cherry, Heartbeat, Higginsville Reader, Midwest Quarterly, Mink Hills Journal, Mockingbird, M.O.O.N., Negative Capability, New Voices (Trinidad and Tobago), *Pacific Coast Review, Pacific Review, Plain Brown Wrapper, Poet Magazine, Potpourri, One Hundred Suns, Outside Lining, Return to Hell, San Miguel Writer* (Mexico), *Santa Barbara Review, Streetfighting Aesthete, Sun Magazine* (Baltimore *Sunday Sun*), *Voices International, Waterways Project, Whiskey Island Magazine, Widener Review, Wild Turkey* (Maverick Press) and *Without Halos*.

"The Great Flood of '93" (under the title "I Woke Up in Platte City") in *Rising Waters*, Walter Bargen and Bob Dyer, editors, Pekitanoui Publications, Boonville, Missouri, 1994.

Bodies of Lightning Copyright © 1995 by Alan Britt. All rights reserved. Printed in the United States of America. No part of this book may be used or reproduced in any manner whatsoever without written permission except in the case of brief quotations embodied in critical articles and reviews. For information address Cypress Books, 1521 Alameda De Las Pulgas, San Mateo, California 94402.

Design by Raphael Diego

Library of Congress preassigned card number: 95-70711

Britt, Alan, 1950--
Bodies of Lightning: poems/Alan Britt

I. Title
811'.54
ISBN: 0-9647754-8-4
First Edition

For my grandfather, Melvin Lee Smith

*My thanks to Herman M. Swafford,
whose encouragement and humanity were invaluable.*

CONTENTS

PART 3
Flying Inside

INTRODUCTION

NAKED IMAGINATION
& THE TWO WORLDS

Bodies of Lightning is a little book comprised of poems from several manuscripts. Poems were chosen because of their affinity with the broad theme of exploration & how imagination moves freely through the inward & outward worlds. Imagination undresses as it prepares to travel.

William Blake really summed it up by saying, "...I Know that This World Is a World of Imagination & Vision...As a man is, So he Sees." Other poets have done a superb job of weaving between the dark world of imagination & the concrete world of broad daylight. Some take legitimate issue with labeling the imagination as "dark", insisting that without imagination sight of any consequence is impossible anyway. Boundaries between external & internal are vague...blurred by emotion & circumstance, desire & need, infatuation & emptiness.

It seems the poem is joy one day & grief the next. Most days it is some place in between. With each occasion a poet's vision is broadened. Each day light grows & darkness bristles. Growth is slow as the cultivation of sensibility occurs by inches in a limitless universe. Vision grows inside an orange or a fist. Poems seem to fall to the floor one by one like the discarded feathers of a soul in flight!

Alan Britt
September 1995

PART 1
The Two Worlds

BODIES OF LIGHTNING

"It is a nameless unhappiness when one's world breaks
in two. O, my God, what a judgement has broken upon me.
Tell me that I must have the strength to stay alive and to do
what is true. Tell me that I am not mad. A stony darkness has
broken upon me."
　　　　　　—Georg Trakl

When one stands in the
　　　　　　　　outer world
one specifically collects the wet feathers
　　　of orchids
from the face of a mirror.

Instantly, when the emotional skin
awakens the new body,
skin that hangs on the body
like a warm breath,
skin that dances naked
　　　　on its nest
　　　　　　　　of bones,
　　the eye then
　　　　of the soul
rotates on its axis
like a sensitive flute
of a deep cello groan.

When one stands in the
　　　　　　　　outer world
one specifically walks
　　　to the edge
of the green window
& gazes inside
　　　at the momentary births
& the stirring of bodies
　　　　made of lightning.

JUST NORTH OF CHARLOTTESVILLE, VIRGINIA

A large, white breasted hawk
on a stubble fence post
leans slightly left
as if falling
& sails low across the highway
barely two car lengths
in front of my bumper
before pouncing on something unseen
in the brown median grass.

As he hits ground
he tumbles almost over,
white underwing
sticking straight up.

His clumsy grace,
it occurs to me,
is precisely that of a poet's
whose inky talons
grasp at a sudden
dark movement
inside a poem.

CROSSING THE WALT WHITMAN BRIDGE

They have named a bridge after Walt.

A massive extension of steel
& persistent weight.

This bridge connects daily lives,
supports the multitudes
nonstop 24 hours a day.

Walt would surely be proud.

But the true bridge,
the one he created
from our lives to the infinite,
is the one I'm crossing now
between the shores of my solitude.

BEAUTIFUL GHOST

I drive to the museum
just to see the Vermeers.

The light that flows
through each of his windows washes
the heavy clothing
& defines the drapery.

Every hand glistens.
All eyes serene & dark.

Each time I stare
into that human light.

Each time I imagine
being touched by the light
feels just like being kissed
by a beautiful ghost!

TRAVELING TO WORK
ONE MORNING IN NOVEMBER

A large owl
sits on the rough branch
of a Virginia pine.

Head turned
far right.

Tawny chest
an oval mantra.

Half a mile away
a sudden splash of orange
among the green pines.

Up ahead
a distant migrating flock
contracts then expands again.

A single hawk
hovers above the expressway.

Maples bleed
in the cold.

I fly
from my windshield
eye to eye with the owl.

The sunlight dapples my clothes
& for a long instant
his eyes are two Saturns
in a new universe.

THE DREAM TYGER

Today is a day for the Dream Tyger
as he moves through Baltimore suburbs
changing his eye color
changing his skin
nourished by the burnt yellow
& the fractured peach
of October elms
but always walking with a limp
it appears
with half a violin
for one leg
hands vibrate in the warm sun
beneath the cold eyelid of religion
that spins our tiny world
in its socket
wearing down the edges
generation by generation

Today the Dream Tyger
barefoot & without commas
nudges through morning foliage
through traffic & horizons of thick smoke
through the blue peeling from the sky
opening the door of one universe
& closing another
if only religions were a waist
as a waist is religion
several religions in fact
sleeping behind a fold of skin
in the Hindu of a smooth shadow
if only the bridge's cold metal
with cakes of rust
would speak openly
to the jetliner headed for Hong Kong
to the boy fast asleep

beneath his pencil lead
& calculator
if only these telephone wires
would become its four birds
at least on rare occasions
like when the teal angel
of the Lord softly displays
her breasts of lightning
on a Thanksgiving table

Are they breasts of delight?

At this moment the Dream Tyger
is a round bush
or a shiny green hedge
that stretches the East Coast
all the way to New York City
preferring the Lincoln Tunnel
(where he sheds a few indiscreet leaves)
& the baked bricks in the walls
where he sleeps in St. Louis San Francisco
& between the cracks
in the borders of California & Mexico
Christ in the eyes of the flowing mountain goat
in Peru & Bolivia
& into the darkness of a wristwatch
the Tyger descends

PHILADELPHIA

Working one spring afternoon
in Mid-Town Philadelphia

with my window
open...in the distance

from exactly which direction
impossible to tell

comes the snakey jazz
of a street player

as his clarinet
inspired from moment to moment

bounces off tall buildings
until it finds

the open mouth
of my tired room.

ONE STEP BEYOND

You take me past common sense. Under
the skin language I understand, but
pure & simple statements of fact...
I hold the dolphin in your hips &
resort to the barebreasted logic of
the infinite when verbs & adjectives
dissolve like cognac on my tongue. I
place words on paper as astral footprints
where there is no body. I don't know
why & that's the gist of it. I don't
know why & that's the fire.

PEGASUS

Solitude with infinite waist
& dark humid mouth
forever out of reach.

I want to awaken
to the snort of Pegasus
in my dimly lit room.

Apollo can wait outside
flirting as usual
with the neighborhood wives,
gazing through every bedroom window
looking sweaty
& forever flexing his undaunted ego.

But upon the back
of his horse of smoke
I want to race —
not through the clouds
as usual
nor through the dreary pages
of American literary genius
but fused as one
determined & reckless
taking direct aim
at the snowy eyes
expanding shoulders
& supple waist
of our unsuspecting infinite!

METAPHYSICAL ANGELS

The metaphysical angels
rise from steam
off the Potomac River

Yellow & orange leaves
words
that burst in the mouth
of a new morning
from this old universe

In a pale gray sweatshirt
I have the waist
of a field mouse

For a single moment
I grow the fish-shaped hands
of an angel!

SOME JANUARY THOUGHTS
OF JUAN RAMON

"...I Know that This World Is a World
of Imagination & Vision...As a man is,
So he Sees."
—William Blake

I love the rain
washed clean,

the white stone
licked by the cow's
tongue
of the dawn.

But walk
walk
down the corridor,
Juan Ramon, of absurd
death.
Walk down the street
of anger.

Down the slope
of a fist
that half-
submerged
resembles your
dark boat.

I love it!

Ah, yes. The boat,
our boat drops
its shadowy anchor
in the depths
of the child,

in the depths
of our eyes
which have been washed
clean once again
like smooth blocks
of salt
licked fresh
by the cow's
tongue
of the dawn.

I love the boat,
Juan Ramon!

Like men
we sink
to our watery depths.

ALMOST ALL ABOUT EYES

"Nanny & Ger have green eyes.
Pop-Pop, Chelsea, Mommy & Daddy
have blue eyes." So says my two
year-old daughter as she looks
up at me...one finger tugging
her eye socket in front of her
crib mirror. She proceeds to give
the two dogs black eyes.

No one ever gave anyone else
a black eye out of innocence, except
Blake when he spoke of his "black-
ey'd maid". I think about how
thrilling it would be to have Blake
here this afternoon...maybe lounging
with a cold one in front of the
storage shed whose door is badly
in need of repair...listening to his
renowned outrageous stories perfectly
fitting for a two & a half year-old
& myself.

Yes, I know having a "cold one"
scoffs literary fashion. But
it's 95 degrees today & who really
cares...whatever suits Blake's fancy
is fine with me...ah, those fanciful
visions he used to share with
Fuseli & Linnell. His tiniest beams
of light that mystified his other
contemporaries who simply waved him
aside fearing possible affliction
from his enlightenment!

What a strange world. What a
world structured by ironies & illusion.

A world where a paradox isn't allowed
the blue-yellow face of a parrot
streaking through the damp shadows
of our emotional jungle...instead
we are more comfortable putting them
each behind bars & covering them
with a sheet at night.

Blue eyes...green eyes...glistening
black agate eyes. The eyes that children
look through & stare back at. The eyes
of innocence, of smoke, of a triangle
with the white face of a clock. The
eyes of an ocean that are always
wet & mysterious...eyelids of
seaweed surrounded by dark shadows
like the young Spanish girl's dreaming
of romance as she sneaks past
the finely trimmed hedges behind
her blue church.

The eyes of mystery...that hold
so much like Marvell's dew drop that
reflects two worlds. Or, with yellow
pollen on his leg, the bee's
eyes that refract the light of angels
near a purple flower. Or the eyes of
pollen for that matter...eyes that
pollinate my daughter causing her
to bloom into a gentle paradox of
imagination!

What color are the eyes?! That
is the question...if you're two
& a half years-old & making glorious

discoveries instead of taking a nap
like you were instructed. The eyes
of sleep are like sheer curtains
or wool blankets...or cold water
with the lips of a deer as he
disappears underneath the crib
into a ball of dust. The eyes of
Tuesday are unlike the eyes of
Saturday but somehow younger than
the eyes of Thursday...or are they
really? Aren't they all really in
the eyes of the beholder...as Tuesday
slips on her light blue dress &
white patent leather shoes to go
out to play?

VAN GOGH

In those paintings about taverns, with
the texture of thick wooden floors, heavy
green-grey bottles, & partial faces...especially
the one with the radiating gas chandelier whose
light resembles fragments of straw that swirl
like abstract angels. With those paintings Vincent
actually created poems...or else we, during
inspired moments, create Van Goghs.

THE FATHER

The father's entire body
is heavy tonight. This father, like all other fathers,
feels lost sometimes. Finding the way back home seems
all too impossible.

I don't remember getting lost.

I clearly remember the infant spark. The brilliance
of my disbelief. I also remember the hours strung
together like a necklace of voices. The days, months,
lifetimes even whizzing by as the automobile splashes
through the street.

Nearby an elm bristles with rain & the
ocean carries the change in our pockets & the plump
hours of our afternoons in its tremendous body. Our
hair feels swept & our bones feel as though they are
made of darkness.

At three years old a face
can shape joy & very quietly absorb neglect into its
shadowy blue eyes. The father drinks every infinitesimal
ounce of the joy & carries every elephant of sadness
inside his stomach.

Fathers, as sure as I am here today, you
fathers of paperweights & fathers of forged tools.
Fathers of white flour on your elbows & fathers of
daily intimidation. All you fathers that sail on ships
& on the thirst for freedom. I say again, I simply
don't remember getting lost.

SARGASSO WEATHER

It's April.

I'm reminded of Eliot.

Inside the airport
thick, dirty clouds
& overpriced, fake bronze souvenirs.

The girl from London
wears a delicate gold chain
around her right thumb.

She wears cowboy boots
& sits apart
from the other British tourists.

It's still April
& the Boeing 737
rocks & vibrates above Baltimore.

Cesar Chavez just died
& we drink chemicals daily.

Our children sip them from bent straws.

I guess it's always April.

There is a scent
on the fingertips of silence.

The scent is blue.

We are cells that float
inside the long shadowy belly
of this airplane.

We float like drops of clear water
in the pale thighs
of celery.

Mumbling.

Hardly audible.

The occasional turn
of the magazine page
draped over a bare knee.

The sargasso lips of a bored afternoon
touch my stomach
as I sway in the infinite hammock.

PART 2

Walking Around

HAVING BREAKFAST WITH A MOCKINGBIRD
NEAR KANSAS CITY, MISSOURI

A few minutes ago, while having breakfast,
at a shaded window-table with coffee & silverware,
still bathing in the afterglow of my metaphorical
tale, pondering still the frailties of the linear
mind, a mockingbird flew straight to my window
& landed at the sill. Stood there looking at me,
with a cricket or two (at least it looked like
two, it was hard to tell) scissored in his thin
beak. He stared through the glass for the longest
time. Several minutes it seemed. How amazing,
I thought, that he would perch before me...jerking
his head slightly from time to time. But then I
wondered if somehow the sun's reflection prevented
him from seeing me through the glass, that maybe
it was his own reflection he was enamoured with.
I couldn't be sure. Behind a small oak our window
was mostly shaded. We were but two feet from
each other...each holding breakfast as our eyes
glistened.

BLACK HORSES

Black horses clump together
near the faded oak fence.

Old snow piled all around them
in the frozen pasture.

Four horses resemble hovering smoke.

Their deep black manes
twitch in the wind's icy fingers.

A SEPTEMBER MORNING IN
MOUNT AIRY, MARYLAND

With a gust
the strong web
shakes its red peach leaves.

Bright sun washes
the entire side of a red barn.

Eleven white cows.
Some in sunlight.
Some in shade.

Rusted tin shed.

Blue road.

Green canvas awnings.

The cold wind smiles
brushing its hips against
the dried blackberry bushes.

A mockingbird sails
across Route 94
to a single tree in a field
asleep with bales of straw.

One thin radio tower
sparks above the pines.

GRANDDAD

Granddad pinches a stalk
off his tomato plant
& loosens the dirt
above its roots.

With hands on his hips
he surveys his woodpile.
The fire that he builds
every December he carries
with him at all times.

The warm tongue of his fire
invariably leaps across the room
chased by his distinctive laugh
that resembles the sound
of a crow swallowing a peacock.

Behind his hazel eyes
lurks the missing two of clubs,
the forgotten card
that stops a run
& fuels a family legend
as it skids into the rest
of the pile
at the center of the table.

Also from his hazel eyes
float the long afternoons
of his life...Through his stories
the years take on shoulders
& a bright red filament that square dances
alone in the darkness.

After final adjustments
he straightens up
takes a half step back
& examines the smooth tomato
cradled in his fingers.
His left sleeve
shields his eyes
& wipes the warm early morning rays
of Indiana sun
from his forehead.

MOTHER & CHILD

In a far off room
I hear my mother reading stories
to my daughter.

A fox in baggy pants,
a muskrat in suspenders,
a frog in a waistcoat.

The pond itself even bristles,
rippling with memories
as fresh as the infant moon.

Our three dogs
walk from one room to another,
following the black wind against the windows
& on the roof.

Light climbs from the top
of the crystal lamp
& breathes in a corner
of the green living room.

Branches creak in the pages
of the storybook.

Imagination flickers
across the dark eyes
of three generations.

TO CHELSEA: ON HER SECOND BIRTHDAY

My little lightning bug,
my ornery peaches & cream.
Chelsea, my little lantern
of dew.

You fill our house
with your incredible innocence
& love twelve different things
a minute.

Even one hundred rooms away
your peppery tears would fly to me
balanced between the striped wings
on the dragonfly of time.

It is not just your eyes
as blue as your delicate madness,
but everything,
you roll your eyes up already
& make comical faces,
you reach out to dance
at the drop of a hat
& you repeat the most peculiar words
at the oddest times.

All I can really say is
the world will simply never be the same.
Even sleep is no longer the same
now that your tiny green flame burns every second
of every day!

WIPING THE STARS

The older Korean gentleman
(barely 55!),
wafer thin,
body slopes like a shoehorn,
drifts across his front lawn
towards the damp curb
at 6:20 A.M.,
chilly March
& misty,
newly lit cigarette
hanging from his mouth,
right hand dangles,
wiping the stars
from his forehead
with his left hand.

ATLANTIC CITY

They arrive by bus.
The retired couple from Bethesda.
A group of young women from Towson
seeking the high life.

Their aspirations severely limited
based solely on two colors: red & black.

Decades ago fifty feet from the boardwalk
the colors were infinite.
The throat of the conch was a shiny pink doorway
to the most sought after apartment
in Atlantic City.

The blue shoulders of the crab
occasionally carried the afternoon fog on his back.
He trailed vanishing hieroglyphics
across the sand's damp eyelashes.
His Dada creations
were truly thrilling.

At midday the wind had solitary lips of coral.

But tonight the guests
see mostly the two colors
with an occasional third one:
the metallic mascara of chance.
Their eyes spiral
as their dreams rattle
& settle upon a number.

In the carnival light of a noisy casino
each card from the blackjack dealer
produces a drug-like high.

So it goes.
In the very early hours of consciousness
innocence is lost & regained many times
underneath the magnetic peanut shell.

STRANGER EYES

A stranger walks over to me
& the eyes are fantastic!
These eyes can look through trees
& can easily pick you apart.
A stranger with eyes like that.
I wonder what she eats for breakfast.

SOUTH MIAMI BEACH

The green humidity
strolls down A1A.

A dead frond lies
against the curb.

The sky
      deep blue
touches the bathers
  terri cloth aliens
    from New Jersey
     Austria
     & Dijon, France.

Six pelicans
  glide overhead
  in a V formation
    before disappearing
   behind the cool palms.

The teeth of the foam
the teeth of the foam
remember the killer hurricane
   that clawed Dade County
   three months ago.

Ah, but the teeth of the foam
now the teeth of the foam
submerge the waist
of a green-eyed saxophone
& swallow the Scandinavian hair
of two strangers.

Soon the night
will part the mimosas
& scoop up the unwitting tourist
inside its belly.

While the moon
the loosely-buttoned, silk-shirted moon
saunters across the sand.
    A sandal flaps
& suddenly the moon
leans on one elbow
at the open-air bar,
turns to the glistening eyes
of the young Cuban girl
seated next to him
& casually offers her a blue drink.

GARDEN SLUG ON A YELLOW SQUASH

I reach through flat leaves
& prickly stalks to capture a pale yellow
squash to steam for the dinner table. Pleased
to still find one in this disheveled September
garden.

Lifting the diminutive
yellow whale to my eyes I notice that its stomach
has long thin splits, with almond-colored spots
beginning to appear. The dirt has already claimed
it! There are a certain number of these gifts
that I simply do not question...knowing they are
bound for earth almost as soon as they emerge.

But this one! Perched on the back of this
lemon-yellow dreaming gourd is a slug...about
the size & shape of my smallest fingertip. Same
shape indeed...almost half head & half body.
Its body portion with the indentations of invisible
scales...a pattern of skin the same as me. With
its back arched & antennae straight out, it peers
at the motion of the world.

Amazed, I stare. A puddle around its
body as it sits peacefully on one end of the
squash. I blow gently on its head & it recoils
instantly...antennae pulled into its head which
is now a nub. Its defense is to be motionless
...withdrawn completely inside its fragile
body...hoping to be overlooked...somehow lost
in a distracting void.

So I respect
this tiny angel...as evening rustles the leaves
...honoring its fragile solitude...by laying the
squash, with its mysterious visitor, on a decaying
mound of grass behind my busy Reisterstown garden!

EARTH MUSIC

I constantly listen to music. Come to
think of it...it drowns out the earth. Don't
hear the earth doing much...mostly yellow
violins, stone pianos & sad guitars. Right
now it's raining. Almost no break in the water
as it dives into the grass outside my lace
window. Actually, the sound is more like palm
fronds blowing in the Cuban wind.

One bubble...one rivulet in the lower
right hand corner of this earth music...where
cool water slides off the back of a ceramic
melancholy at the end of a drain pipe. Thunder
rolls slowly over the rough shingles of this
house.

Earth music. Do you hear it?

THE GRASSHOPPER & THE MOWER,
OR, THE MOWER'S SONG

"And thus, ye meadows, which have been
Companions of my thoughts more green,
Shall now the heraldry become
With which I shall adorn my tomb;
For Juliana comes, and she,
What I do to the grass, does to my thoughts and me."
    —Andrew Marvell

Wet cinnamon body...
Dark banded thighs...

I stopped the mower,
seeing you atop thick grass,
cradled you in my heavily gloved hands
& began to carry you toward a nearby spruce.
Suddenly you fluttered from my leathery palm
& landed on a low spruce branch.
It was there that I closely examined
the dark wide bands that ran
from your knees to your upper thighs.

With you perched on a tuft of bluegreen needles
we stared eye to eye
as the nearby mower roared
& devoured fuel
our eyes devoured space
& the strangeness of our alien species.

You sat on that branch for a few minutes,
then in an instant disappeared
into the white-gloved afternoon's slight-of-hand!

I uprighted my stance
& moved for the next hour

with dark banded thighs of my own
for all the neighbors to see
from their open September windows.

IN THE WHITENESS

(For Christina Orman Senior)

In the whiteness of snow
death comes.

In the absence of pain,
uttering barely audible sentences.

It takes us for granted,
but took you from us.

It came with a face
that was hardly a face at all

& eased a hand
gently beneath your back.

It put out the lamp
& turned off the stove

& refused to reheat
the left-over turkey

& inevitably left some
words unsaid.

Death fell from the folds
in your apron

but we didn't even notice it,
had no idea.

I know death comes
to the strangest places

at the strangest times.
Sometimes it moves right in

& takes up residence,
other times it doesn't even

bother to knock.
But when I actually held it

last summer by its roots
in my gardening glove,

I didn't know
what I had.

I never realized
that you & death,

strolling arm in arm,
would soon become a couplet.

WALKING NEAR VIRGINIA BEACH

Motionless in a pool of water
a yellow-billed crane
like a white knife leans into the wind.

The silence nearby
puts on a blue dress.

Suddenly lifts itself
into the afternoon
dragging me behind
inside the violin bones
of its dark legs!

A CROWD OF MAPLE TREES

A crowd of maple trees
pumps the red into its leaves.

An astral red,
a wine-colored red
more profuse than Crashaw's fountain,
more immediate than classical angels.

A red that heals
the carved waistline of a woods.

Makes the woods bristle.

Reddens the roots
of a hundred gods
that rinse their backbones
in the cold blue air.

ON A FOGGY MORNING

The two white bands
on the mockingbird's outstretched wings

cut the heavy fog
with the magnesium light

of a new savior.

THE PARROT TREES

The road is chilly

An October breeze
rubs its belly
against some rusty branches

A dark violin
rests behind the yellow leaves
of an oak

As I rise & dip
with the highway
the single hawk
tilted against a cloud

But just ahead, for miles,
huge golden feathers,
many green
on either side,
& sudden patches
of red
tucked beneath the lower cheeks
of at least
one thousand parrot trees

THE GREAT FLOOD OF '93

I woke up in Platte City, Missouri this
morning. The flood waters recede a little more
each day. On the news, Baby Jessica was pulled
from the arms of her Michigan mother & father,
from her toy-covered, yellow bedroom & handed
over to her estranged biological family. It broke
her heart. Her broken heart broke mine.

A picture of flames engulfing another village
shelled by Serbs. I hardly notice, though I know
I should. Every day the shelling goes on. In
Yugoslavia, the Middle East, somewhere in Central
or South America, Los Angeles or D.C. The brutality
of the moment has us all cut by shards of hatred,
by the vulgarity of indifference. Luis Cernuda
wrote: "The revolution is always reborn, like a
phoenix/Flaming in the breast of the wretched./
Underneath the trees of the plaza the charleton/
Knows this, drooling silver, ringing his bell,/
Whistling among the leaves, he delights/The robust
townspeople with malignant eloquence,/and songs
of blood rock misery to sleep."

Here in the hotel room the vacuum hums...
the air conditioner exhales. The ice sinks periodically
in its bucket. I have come to the conclusion that
most of the world, as we know it, is constantly
fighting off a feeling of misery. Misery heavily
punctuated as in Yugoslavia, or along New York
Avenue in D. C. Misery that goes unrecognized
or that is avoided, as by the IBM workaholic. The
misery of wading in hip boots through your living
room or watching your house slowly spin as it
floats down river. The misery of judges ordering

you to leave your yellow bedroom & familiar voices
of your mother & father forever. Your
little tears cannot stop your misery, though through
them your house too floats away spinning counter
clockwise from your memory.

Our memory is indeed a great flood, but not
of 1993, or '94 or 1893 & so on. (Of course, there
is no such thing as collective sorrow, only individual
misery squared & cubed out of control.) Our
individual misery is probably inherited, continually
passed down through our chromosomes, buried in
the recesses of our DNA. So when the judges
roll up their sleeves & sandbag the Mississippi,
when the Serbian with a microscope for an eye
begins to meticulously rearrange the tiny strands
of his sensibility, humanity will change just a
little. Misery, as we know it, may even decline
by a few decimal points.

Misery will never go away, though. In the
heaven we have created, the angels are miserable
because we are constantly tearing the place up,
sailing paper stealth bombers across the room
towards the new boy with black hair & funny
looking glasses. The angels are miserable because
we never seem to get beyond the fifth grade,
& so continuing in their infinite wisdom, to
encourage our correct behavior, they scold us
with stories of the really Great Flood, the one
that is yet to come.

PART 3

Flying Inside

A LITTLE POEM ABOUT DARKNESS
& A DRIVER

Darkness everywhere,
in his voice,
in his eyes,
in the skin on his face
darkness breeds a separate universe.

He feels darkness
on the swirled tips of his fingers
as he dreams a white paradox.

Extending his arms
beyond the aging dashboard
he lifts one orange pumpkin
from a careless pile
crowded into the bed
of an open truck as it hurries
along a Virginia highway.

The smooth, bumpy skin
leaves its orange light
on both palms of his hands.

For just a single moment
the road is infinite.

WOODEN MOON

The wooden moon
is a drifter.
Hangs his hat
on any tree.

Rattles the cages
of my daughter's blue eyes.

Takes up residence
in the long strands of our loneliness.

CUBAN DREAM

1.

My shadow carries a sponge
down the beach.

2.

Rosa Maria brings us coffee
in small cups.

She has never left the island.

The coffee glistens the color of her eyes.

3.

A thousand mangrove roots
pull us beneath the water.

4.

Green water.

Large waves with muscular hips.

5.

A humid wind washes us to our bones.

AN ANGEL & THE BIRDS OF PARADOX

1.

Logic places barbed wire
around an angel
The imagination makes him
invisible to barbed wire
Makes him glow
deep red
Gives him eyes which are punctuation
marks for the universe
Gives him hair from Monet's
paint brush
Lips shaped like a dark bird
Hands of blue dolphins
& infant feet which slowly
begin to resemble a bottle
of spilled wine

2.

Logic purses its lips
Itself with a thousand teeth
& a digestive tract as long
as history

3.

A child plays in the cold afternoon
Her shrieks of laughter
are sudden birds
The closer she gets
the more I hear the birds of paradox

GRIEF

Grief. I absorb it
like a sponge.

Today I do.

Tomorrow I won't.
Tomorrow I'll be as hard as wood.

Children abducted. Missing.
Stolen by thieves who
should never be set free
to brutalize a second time.

Tonight a baby poisoned
by its mother.

Tomorrow, a brother,
a sister, a wife.

Dark birds fly overhead
dispersing grief.

In the shiny eyes
of these dark birds
their delicate light is a mantra
for our grief...a thin
wafer of deepest sorrow.

In the hollow bones
of the green wind, there
is a constant tapping,
a sound that almost resembles birth.

THE TRAIL OF TEARS

Who can imagine this prejudice with hands
larger than the universe? A cruelty unfit for any
life form? It was an eviction of souls followed by
a looting that wasn't obliged to stop with the
bones of the dead.

Even as the Land of Opportunity raised its
flags on courthouse steps, the heavy wagons with their
ironic wheels failed to crush the Baptist blood
of the Cherokees. & within this religious aberration
the genocide was already well underway...for now the
stars on rusty pulleys were being hauled by machines
across the sky.

Some elderly, barefooted, & infants in gowns
of cholera fell hourly into the teeth of the infinite.
Death, you see, was something more than just a thief
of possessions, but with fist raised in robe of stars
& stripes was the absolute dictator of misery. & as
each body littered the earth like a trail of bread crumbs
towards oblivion, the wind followed along perfectly
behind scattering their bones like dried seeds.

Amazing to think so many years later that the
handed down stories can still locate some footprints
left in the snow & dust. & in the frozen hand of grief
those tears & groans that once were squeezed so
tightly...now form fine beads of sweat above the
adolescent lips of the Cherokee girl kneeling today
at mass.

OCELOT SONATA

Large rain drops
spot the foggy windshield.

I stare at the ocelot sky.
It stares back,
rubs its loose body
against my chest.

Its eyes are lanterns
that sound like golden violins.

It stretches across
an overpass
allowing its long tail
to brush the tops
of several thousand
wet & lonely cars.

A FEW MINUTES AGO I SPOKE
TO THE MAN IN THE TALL GRASS

The man in the tall grass
said he didn't want to live.

Had no mother or father
& didn't know how to live,

didn't know love,
thought kisses were house flies.

The man in the tall grass
saw his sister bruised

by a brutish husband,
her children frightened,

their eyes forever lowered like two
Chinese servants offering silk pillows

for the Emperor. The man
lies down in the tall grass,

says some days he feels
like the green parakeet

his grandmother kept for years
by the dining room window.

The parakeet had committed no crime.
The man in the tall grass

never understood the silver teeth
of darkness that closed

like iron gates on the footsteps of Hansel
and his sister, Gretel.

Dreams he is weeping
but doesn't know why,

doesn't understand why
his soul feels like a paper nest

built by wasps,
or why the thin waist

of just one wasp
resembles the voice

of his lover.

THREE-LEGGED HORSE

All day long I've been going
in fits & starts.
Just when I get moving
something slips inside
& I go under.
I need a jump-start
from my guardian angel
but I haven't seen him/her
for so long,
I believe the heavenly real estate deal
in Barbados must've worked out
with Margaritas on the veranda,
stars the size of cocktail napkins,
and a warm breeze under the skin.
There are no phones
so I can't call,
no TV
so I can't advertise.
I need my boots
so I can plant a heavy foot
on the road,
find my balance
so I can kiss misery
square on the lips.
Maybe I'll buy a six-gun
so I can shoot my way out.
That's it!
Enough of this,
I'm ready to move.
Where's my three-legged horse?

THE BEAST

When the beast wakes up
it'll know exactly where to go
& what to do.

If I don't know which way
to turn
buttoning my sleeves of confusion
I summon the beast.

The beast could tear through a window
or hallucinate a moon
or sip cabernet from an ultra thin wine glass
tilted backwards in the most delicate manner
in a hand that is more like an orchid
growing from the end of a black gown.

The darkness in my room
has the voice of white dogwood
& a silk scarf tied around its thigh.

If I can't find the door
it's because the beast has hidden it
inside its perfumed mouth
behind its lips which blow the twelve dark kisses
of a paradox.

The shine on its boot is the tongue of a streetlight.

The slant of its eye is a soprano's knife
wrapped in silk.

A romance that is not a romance
but the tease of an eternal day

an impossible hour.

I watch the morning pull its hair back
in a knot of despair.

The beast can be very simple.

It can come & go like a cough.

It can pull a coin from my pocket
& toss it into the lusty mouth
of the infinite.

Or it can simply pin a note
to my sleeping pulse
saying that time is so relative
I'd better hurry
if I'm ever going to find this thief
who lifted my dreaming Muse
from its moonlit casket.

FLOATING MISTRESS

Far from philosophies,
I travel with my mistress, imagination.

We spend the night
in a tavern lit by gas chandeliers.

Van Gogh appears
to be sitting across from us,
head supported by one hand.

Women & men in complete freedom
circle the tables.

No police,
no governments,
no ministers.

Together we sip
& chat with Jeanne Duvall,
whose careless arm tilts,
then Degas walks in
followed by a woman with a green hand.

For an hour
that lasts a year
or four seconds.

I rise up
on the lips of absinthe,
completely enslaved by your reckless eyes.

NEEDLE

Now that's something.
The saxophone
leaves an echo
like a handprint on your mouth.
The cats are huddled
near the electric heating vents
or else in your bed.

I am as far away
as a needle
leaving its first stitch.

MEMORIES

All that can be said
is that the memories fly
their roots dangle
& touch my arm
like electric wires

Today a rose grows from the telephone

Some memories are etched
in the lines below your brow
& I see myself parked at night
headlights dimmed
on the surface of your eyes

It's hard to talk about such things
but more difficult to keep quiet
so I take the days
one by one
as though they were pages
turning below my skin

RILKE SKY

There are three layers of dusk.

October with a horn of sexual ivory.

The powder, of course, is useless.

The angels are violins
for one hour.

SIDEWINDER'S ADAGIO

i

The distance
    between
rhetoric & the bumble bee's heavy body
is exactly one mile.

The bee
    shifts
  his weight
at the opening of the lilac-colored blossom.

    Head first
        into the dark throat
   of a few seconds,
       into the dark voice
  of an hour
       that is circular
        its ragged edges
gradually vanishing completely.

ii

In the distance Haydn
is playing

    .

  .

 .

    violins
   darting their heads
in an 18th Century
    mating ritual.

On the Mojave
   rattlesnakes
curl around the moon's nest

...the sidewinder's adagio
leaves no echo
down the long hallways of the Senate Building.
Congressmen mill around
with file folders
under their arms
heads tilted back
            waltzing with reporters
                        & staff.

            iii

A trestle bridge
stretches
            across a highway
so conveniently
the bridge goes nowhere
in either direction.

            iv

A cello concerto
about the size of a hand
leans to one side
like a Picasso woman
                  w
                   i
                    t
                     h
                  one eye
            & lowered shoulder.

The distance
        between the cello's strings
is the distance inside a mouth.

The distance
        inside melancholy
  is immeasurable.

CATARACT MOON

"You have about as much chance as
a laboratory rat," she crooned, whose eyes,
I once read, are wine colored. The eyes,
on closer inspection, become Spanish and
glisten with overwhelming sadness as the rat
paces behind his tiny bars. I pace with
him behind my bars of manhood, stepping
over remnants of newspaper & bits of wood
chips when we're lucky enough to have
all natural floors.

We wait for injections into the
abdomen or cancer behind the ear to develop
on schedule. We are so disappointed when
we survive.

I have about as much chance as a
creature whose bones are made of moonlight
& whose claws are the tiny claws of the
infinite as they scratch out a code, a poem,
on the fire-bright pages of my soul.

A yellow cab with red fenders drives
off a discarded calendar in the attic &
picks us up at a snowy curbside. We travel
through the dark, through the electric
arteries of swan-neck streetlights. I & the
rat with wine colored eyes...we both with
a swollen ear...lanced by the rays of a
cataract moon.

From left to right: Aunt Glenda, Alan,
Granddad Melvin and Grandmother Vida.